The Angel of Goliad

Francisca Alvarez and the Texas War for Independence

Joanne Randolph

ROSEN CENTRAL

PRIMARY SOURCE™

THE ROSEN PUBLISHING GROUP, INC., NEW YORK

Published in 2004 by The Rosen Publishing Group, Inc.
29 East 21st Street, New York, NY 10010

Editor: Scott Waldman
Book Design: Erica Clendening
Photo researcher: Rebecca Anguin-Cohen

*Thanks to Newton M. Warzecha, Director of Presidio La Bahia, and Mary Livingston, Historic Sites Manager,
Goliad State Park, for their assistance.*

Photo Credits: Cover (left), title page, p. 30 courtesy of Phillip C. Tucker III Papers, The
Center for American History, The University of Texas at Austin, CN 11561; cover (right)
illustration © Debra Wainwright/The Rosen Publishing Group; p. 6
provided courtesy of Presidio La Bahia, Goliad, Texas; pp. 10, 29 The Dallas Historical
Society; p. 14 courtesy of Texas State Library and Archives Commission; p. 18 courtesy of
Mission Espiritu Santo, Goliad State Park, Texas Parks and Wildlife Department, photo by
Dallas Hoppestad; p. 22 Presidio La Bahia, Goliad, Texas, photo by Dallas Hoppestad; pp. 31
Institute for Texan Culture at UTSA (68-2889); p. 32 The San Jacinto Museum of History,
Houston, Texas

First Edition

Publisher Cataloging Data

Randolph, Joanne
  The Angel of Goliad : Francisca Alvarez and the Texas War for Independence / Joanne Randolph.
  p. cm. — (Great moments in American history)
  Summary: Francisca Alvarez, traveling with her husband who was a Mexican army
  officer, saves the lives of twenty captured Texan soldiers in Goliad, Texas.
  ISBN 0-8239-4350-X (lib. bdg.)
  1. Alavez, Francisca—Juvenile literature   2. Goliad \ Massacre, Goliad, Tex., 1836—
    Juvenile literature   3. Texas—History—Revolution, 1835-1836—Juvenile literature
  4. Women heroes—Texas—Goliad—Biography—Juvenile literature 5. Women—
  Mexico—Biography—Juvenile literature [1. Alavez, Francisca   2. Goliad Massacre,
  Goliad, Tex., 1836   3. Women heroes   4. Mexicans—Texas   5. Women—
  Biography 6. Texas—History—Revolution, 1835-1836]   I. Title II. Series 2004

  976.4'03—dc21
  [B]   2003-007574

Manufactured in the United States of America

CONTENTS

Preface

*I*n 1835, Texas was a part of Mexico. However, many Texans wanted to form their own country. They did not want to be a part of Mexico. By the next year, the Texans had set up their own government and said that they were now independent. The Mexican government, led by General Antonio Lopez de Santa Anna, did not want the Texans to become independent. Santa Anna sent soldiers to fight with the Texans. The war that started became known as the Texas War of Independence.

One of the most famous battles of the war happened at the Alamo in San Antonio, Texas. The Alamo was an old mission that was being used as a fort by Texan soldiers and their supporters. On March 6, 1836, the fighting ended. In a battle that lasted twelve days, the Texans had fought

against almost four thousand Mexican soldiers. About 183 Texans were killed. At that point in the war, the Mexican army seemed to be winning.

Francisca Alvarez was the wife a Mexican army officer who was serving under General Jose Urrea. She stayed with the Mexican army as it traveled through Mexico and Texas. Alvarez saw many battles between Texans and Mexicans. She took care of many wounded soldiers from both sides. Three weeks after the battle at the Alamo, she saved the lives of twenty captured Texan soldiers in the town of Goliad, Texas. The soldiers were to be killed by the Mexican troops that caught them.

Her bravery earned her the name of the Angel of Goliad. However, Francisca Alvarez was really only doing what she had always done—helping people who were in need.

General Jose Urrea spent most of his life on the battlefield. In 1846, he would lead the Mexican troops against the United States in the Mexican-American War.

Chapter One

MARCHING WITH THE MEXICAN ARMY

I t was March 18, 1836. Under the command of General Jose Urrea, the Mexican army, had spent most of March on the move through Texas. The soldiers had Texan prisoners with them who were captured in battle. For days, heavy rains had soaked everyone on the march. Francisca Alvarez pulled her wool coat tightly around her head. She kept looking back at the cart in which the Texans were being carried. The prisoners had been shot in a recent battle. Francisca was worried that their wounds would become infected if the rain didn't stop. Her husband, Captain Telesforo Alvarez, didn't seem to be worried about the prisoners. He spent most of the day riding up and down among the marching Mexican army, yelling orders at the officers.

Francisca was used to traveling for long periods of time with the Mexican army, marching from one battle to another. They would march all day long, no matter what the weather was like. When they stopped for the night, everyone hurried to set up camp before dark fell. Then they'd have just enough time to cook dinner. After that, all were so tired, they'd fall right into bed. The next morning, they'd wake up to a bugle call as the sun rose and begin another long day.

Francisca hated the battles. All day long, she would hear the sounds of cannons firing and men screaming in pain. She would rush about, trying to help all the wounded Mexican soldiers. Sometimes, she even helped the wounded Texan prisoners. Her husband did not like her helping the prisoners. "Why are you trying to heal our enemies?" he would ask angrily. "Don't you know that the Texans want to break away from Mexico? They are trying to split apart our country!"

Francisca never paid attention to her husband when he scolded her for helping wounded men. When she saw people in pain, she didn't care what side they were on. She treated their wounds. The men were very thankful to have Francisca with them. She was also one of the few people traveling with the Mexican army who could speak English to the Texan prisoners.

For days, some of the other officers' wives had been talking about a battle with Texans at Fort Goliad. On March 18, General Urrea was at the front of the Mexican troops, just outside the desert. He was talking with some of his men. They were all looking toward Fort Goliad and pointing to a stretch of desert behind it. In the old fort, Texans were getting together all their supplies so that they could march the next day. Francisca had a feeling that soon she would have plenty of wounded soldiers and prisoners to look after.

Colonel James Fannin had a hard time making decisions. If he had decided to leave Goliad earlier, he might not have been captured and killed by General Urrea.

Chapter Two

BATTLE AT COLETO CREEK

General Urrea looked at the strip of desert behind the fort. If the Texans were leaving Goliad, he figured they would be making their way back to the Alamo. After quietly staring at the desert for a few minutes, he turned to a few of the Mexican officers with him. "We'll let them go out into the desert," he said. "Tomorrow, when they have no chance of escape, we'll attack." The officers returned to the rest of the men and told them of the plan.

That night, Francisca could not sleep. All night long, she thought about all the injured men she would have to take care of the next day. She knew that many men sleeping in her camp would wake up the next morning for the last time in their lives.

When the bugle sounded at 4 A.M. on March 19, Francisca quickly got dressed. Captain Alvarez was already up and dressed. Within an hour, he and the other officers had their men lined up for battle. They began the long march across the desert toward the Texans. A group of Mexican soldiers rode ahead on horseback. They rushed toward the Texans. Their plan was to fight the Texans until the Mexican soldiers marching on foot caught up. The Texans were moving very slowly because they were carrying many heavy guns and supplies.

The leader of the Texans, Colonel James Fannin, noticed Mexican soldiers in the distance, racing toward him on horseback. He ordered his four hundred men to form into a square shape. That way, they could fight off an attack from all sides. The Texans stopped in a

flat area near Coleto Creek. Since there were no trees or rocks to hide behind, the fight would have to take place on open ground. The Mexican soldiers on horseback started firing as soon as they got close enough. The Battle of Coleto Creek had begun.

Even though Francisca was a few miles from the fight, she could hear the sounds of guns and cannons being fired. A thick cloud of smoke formed over the battle. She set up an area where she could safely take care of wounded soldiers. All day long, men were brought to her on horse-drawn carts. The Mexican soldiers marching on foot joined the fight that evening. Now, there were about one thousand Mexican soldiers at the battle. Even though the Texan soldiers were very brave, Francisca wondered if any of them would live to see another day.

When the Texan soldiers were captured, they were taken to this fort. Once there, they were not given much food or water. Many of them were not treated for their wounds.

TAKING PRISONERS OF WAR

When night fell, the fighting stopped. Francisca hoped that the Texan soldiers would leave in the night so that the battle would end. However, when the sun rose the next morning, she saw that Fannin and his soldiers had not left. Francisca sighed. *These men will not escape with their lives*, she thought. *Boom!* A cannon fired by the Mexican army jarred her from her thoughts. The Mexican army began another attack upon the Texans.

After an hour or so, the Texans held up a large white flag and began to wave it. The flag meant that they were giving up. This pleased Francisca. She wanted to see the Texans taken as prisoners and not cut down in the battlefield. No more shots were fired. Three Mexican officers rode over to the

15

Texans to speak with Colonel Fannin. When the officers rode back, they spread the word that the Texans had agreed to stop fighting. The Texans were to turn over their guns to the Mexicans. In return, they wanted to be let go in a few weeks.

Francisca watched as the Mexican army took the Texans' guns away from them. Then all the Texan soldiers were lined up and made to march toward Fort Goliad. "What will become of these men?" she asked an officer.

"They are enemies of Mexico and will be treated as such," he replied.

"What are you going to do with them?" Francisca asked.

"The next couple of days will decide that," answered the officer as he turned away.

The officer walked over to a man getting ready to ride away on his horse. The officer gave the man a piece of paper. The man rode away quickly. Francisca knew that the rider was a messenger.

He was taking the news that the Mexicans had won the battle to General Santa Anna. General Santa Anna was in charge of the entire Mexican army. He hated Texans and often treated them very badly. Sometimes he ordered his men to shoot the Texan prisoners. Francisca worried about what might happen to the prisoners.

Just then her husband came up to her and told her that he was taking her to Fort Goliad. She was going to be helping Mexican soldiers who had been wounded in the battle. Francisca climbed onto the back of his horse. When they reached the fort, she saw that all the Texan prisoners were being forced into an old church. Many men had been crowded into the church. They did not even have enough room to sit down. The Mexicans wheeled a large cannon in front of the door. Next to the cannon stood a man with a torch. If any of the prisoners tried to get out of the church, the cannon would be fired at them.

Francisca helped take care of all the prisoners while they were captured. Years after the war was over, she was upset that she wasn't able to help save more men. This painting of Francisca was done in a church near Goliad, Texas so that her brave acts will never be forgotten.

Chapter Four

TIME IS RUNNING OUT

Francisca could not sleep for the next few days. She spent her time treating wounded Mexican soldiers. She saw that the Texans who had been wounded were not being taken care of. The doctors for the Texan army were being forced to care for the Mexican prisoners. Many Texan soldiers who had been shot in the battle of Coleto Creek were dying because they had no doctors to look after them.

"Have the prisoners been given water?" Francisca asked a soldier.

"You should not worry so much about the enemies of Mexico," replied the soldier.

"They can't go long without water. It's very hot inside that church," she said.

"Pretty soon, they'll have more to worry about than whether or not they have water," said the soldier.

"What do you mean?" asked Francisca, her voice cracking with fear. The officer walked away, quietly saying something about Santa Anna's orders.

The prisoners were finally allowed to come out of the church. The Texans were given raw meat to eat. They quickly started fires and began cooking the meat.

Francisca went over to check on some of the prisoners. Their hands and feet were tied with rope. The rope was so tight, the men could not move their hands or feet. Francisca ordered some nearby Mexican soldiers to cut the ropes off of the men's hands. Then she had water brought to them. Since her husband was an officer of the Mexican army, no one questioned Francisca's orders.

That night Francisca heard people talking outside of her tent. She got out of bed and crept

closer to hear what they were saying. She heard that a man had just come into the camp with a message from General Santa Anna. General Urrea was no longer in command. Santa Anna did not feel that Urrea would be able to carry out his orders. So he had sent another man, Colonel José Nicolás de la Portilla, to take charge. Santa Anna wanted all of the prisoners to be killed the next morning. Colonel Portilla was there to make sure it happened.

Then Francisca came up with an idea: She would hide as many men as she could that night. Without wasting any time, she took a few of the Texan doctors and told them to hide in her tent. Francisca knew that if she got caught she would be killed. She gathered a few prisoners and told them about a place in the fort where they would not be seen. Then Francisca got a Mexican army officer to help her hide a few more men before the sun rose. It was only a matter of hours before the shooting began.

This modern painting was made by Frances Ann Vykoukal. It shows Francisca Alvarez with Mexican General Urrea's wife saving the life of young Benjamin Franklin Hughes.

Chapter Five

GUNSHOTS AT GOLIAD

At dawn the next morning, the prisoners were all awakened. The Texans who had been injured were told to stay in the fort. The others were told that they had a few minutes to get their belongings. Then they were formed into two long lines. A Mexican army officer gave the order for the prisoners to start marching. Many of the prisoners were happy. They thought that they were finally being allowed to go home. However, they did not notice that the Mexican soldiers had no supplies for a long trip. All the soldiers carried were guns that had bayonets attached.

Francisca stood quietly watching. As the group went by, she grabbed a young Texan out of the line. His name was Benjamin Franklin Hughes

and he was only fifteen years old. He was a drummer, not a soldier. Hughes was to march ahead of the Texan army and play the drums. Francisca told him to stay next to her. When a Mexican soldier tried to stop her, she slapped his hand away. She reminded him that she was the wife of a Mexican officer. The soldier quickly walked away.

When the prisoners had marched for a few minutes, they were told to stop. The Mexican soldiers split the Texans into three groups. Each group was marched in a different direction for about a minute. Again they were told to stop. The Mexican soldiers formed a line next to them. The prisoners figured out what was happening. They put up their hands and asked to be spared. The Mexican soldiers raised their guns and waited for their orders.

Crack! Hundreds of Mexican soldiers fired at the prisoners. Most of the prisoners died instantly. Then the Mexican soldiers rushed at them and killed the rest with their bayonets.

Over 340 Texans would be killed. Francisca hurried back into the fort, crying.

Francisca saw a soldier holding two of the Texan doctors she had hidden in her tent.

"What were these men doing in your tent?" the soldier asked. He raised his gun at the men, preparing to shoot them.

"No!" screamed Francisca. She ran in front of the prisoners. "You must shoot me before you shoot these men!"

Francisca did not move. The soldier put down his gun. He walked away, shaking his head. Francisca quickly gathered the other men she had hidden during the night. There were twenty of them. She knew that soon the rest of the Mexican soldiers would return to the fort. She gave each prisoner a canteen full of water and told them the way back to Texas.

They thanked her for her kindness. They called her the Angel of Goliad because she had not let them die. The prisoners knew that by saving them, Francisca was putting her own

life in danger. They hurried away from the fort before the Mexicans discovered that they were still alive.

Francisca kept Benjamin Franklin Hughes with her. She did not want to risk having anything happen to him. Hughes traveled with Francisca and her husband when they left the fort. Her husband was angered by what Francisca had done. He could not understand why she would help the enemies of Mexico. He did not speak to her for days.

A few months later, Francisca's husband left her. He hated Texans and would not be married to a woman who felt sorry for them. Francisca was left with no money and no home. Still, she continued to care for Texan prisoners wherever she went. Francisca didn't care what side people were on in the war. When they needed help, she helped them. She will always be remembered in history as the Angel of Goliad.

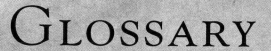

GLOSSARY

battle (BAT-uhl) a fight between two armies

bayonet (BAY-uh-net) a long knife that can be fastened to the end of a rifle

enemies (EH-uh-meez) countries or armies fighting against each other in a war

government (GUHV-urn-muhnt) the people who rule or govern a country or state

heal (HEEL) to cure someone or make the person healthy

independence (in-di-PEN-duhnss) to be free from the control of other people or things

infected (in-FEK-TED) to have gotten an illness caused by germs or viruses

mission (MISH-uhn) a church or other place where people from a religious group live and work

officer (OF-uh-sur) someone who is in charge of other people

prisoners (PRIZ-uhn-urz) people who have been captured or are held

wounded (WOON-dehd) to have been hurt in an accident or because of violence

PRIMARY SOURCES

We can learn about the people, places, and events of long ago by studying primary sources. Primary sources are materials such as letters, paintings, photographs, diaries, and maps. For example, by analyzing the painting of the battle at the Alamo on page 31, we can identify how battles were often fought at the time of Francisca Alvarez. Guns were less powerful and less accurate than they are today, so soldiers usually had to fight each other at very close range.

Studying primary sources can also help us identify a person's point of view about a historic event. The letter on page 30 was written by Benjamin Franklin Hughes, the fifteen-year-old who was was saved by Alvarez. In the letter, we learn what Hughes was thinking and feeling at the time of his rescue. Studying sources such as the painting and the letter help us to understand events that happened many years ago.

Unlike most of the men at Goliad, these men escaped and lived long lives. They lived to see Texas become a part of the United States.

Benjamin Franklin Hughes, who was saved from death by Francisca Alvarez, wrote this letter (also shown on cover) about what happened at Goliad. In it, he tells his own story of that day and the actions taken by Francisca.

The Mexican army under General Santa Anna killed almost everyone at the Alamo a few weeks before Goliad. Many people in the United States were very upset by this. About ten years later, Mexico and the United States went to war.

General Santa Anna worried that the United States would come to the aid of the Texans. He ordered the killings at Goliad as well as the Alamo to scare Texans. Instead, these acts made people in the United States want to go to war with Mexico.